What
Weather Today?

by Pat Cusick

HOUGHTON MIFFLIN BOSTON

Look at the sky.
It is cloudy.

Look at the sky.
It is rainy.

Look at the sky.
It is windy.

Look at the sky.
It is snowy.

Look at the sky.
It is stormy.

Look at the sky.
It is foggy.

Look at the sky.
It is sunny.